FRONTIER LAND

EXPLORERS

OF THE FRONTIER

Charles W. Sundling

Visit us at
www.abdopub.com

Published by ABDO Publishing Company, 4940 Viking Drive, Edina, MN 55435.

Printed in the United States.

Edited by: Tamara L. Britton
Art Direction: John Hamilton

Cover photo: Corbis-Bettmann
Interior photos: Corbis-Bettmann

Sources: Adams, Alexander B. *Sunlight and Storm: The Great American West.* New York: Putnam and Sons, 1977; *American Heritage History of the Great West, The.* New York: American Heritage, 1965; Baker, Daniel B. *Explorers & Discoverers of the World.* Detroit: Gale Research, 1993; Bohlander, Richard. *World Explorers & Discoverers.* New York: MacMillan Publishing Co., 1992; Davis, Nora Deakin. *The Father of Waters.* Sierra Club Books, 1982; DeVoto, Bernard. *Across the Wide Missouri.* Boston: Houghton Mifflin, 1947; Encarta 98 Desk Encyclopedia, 1996-97, Microsoft Corporation, 1996; Encyclopedia Britannica, Chicago: Encyclopedia Britannica, Inc., 1993; Grolier Multimedia Encyclopedia, The 1995, Grolier Electronic Publishing, 1995; Lamar, Howard (editor). *The Reader's Encyclopedia of the Old West.* New York, 1977; Lund, Duane R. *Our Historic Upper Mississippi.* Cambridge: Adventure Publications, 1991; Milner, Clyde A. et. al. (editors). *The Oxford History of the American West.* New York, 1990; Rawling, Gerald. *The Pathfinders.* New York: MacMillan and Co., 1964.

Library of Congress Cataloging–in–Publication Data

Sundling, Charles W.
    Explorers of the frontier / Charles W. Sundling
      p. cm. — (Frontier land)
    Includes index.
    Summary: Describes the efforts of such men as Coronado, de Soto, Drake, and, in particular, Lewis and Clark to search for what came to be known as the Northwest Passage.
    ISBN 1-57765-044-1
    1. West (U.S.)—Discovery and exploration—Juvenile literature. 2. Explorers—West (U.S.)—History—Juvenile literature. 3. Frontier and pioneer life—West (U.S.)—Juvenile literature. [1. Explorers. 2. West (U.S.)—Discovery and exploration. 3. Lewis and Clark Expedition (1804-1806)] I. Title. II. Series: Sundling, Charles W. Frontier land.
F592.S6495S86 2000
978'.01—dc21
                                      98-18685
                                      CIP

Second printing 2002   AC

CONTENTS

A living history program relives the life and times of the 1800s for visitors to the Fort Clatsop National Memorial in Oregon. A staff member dressed in 1800s period clothing stands by a log dugout canoe near the fort built by explorers Lewis and Clark.

CITIES AND GOLD

In 1540, Francisco Vasquez de Coronado, the 30-year-old governor of New Spain (which is now Mexico), led a group of explorers north. Coronado's group wanted to search the land north of the Rio Grande River. They were looking for the fabled "Seven Cities of Cibola," cities so rich that the people paved the streets with gold.

Coronado's group first arrived in what is now the state of New Mexico. They met a group of Native Americans called

Francisco Vasquez de Coronado sets out with men and horses in search of legendary cities of great wealth.

the Zunis. Coronado soon learned, however, that the Zunis were not the people of the Seven Cities of Cibola. They lived in villages, with no golden streets. In fact, the Zunis had little wealth. Coronado decided that the seven cities of gold must be a myth—they didn't really exist.

Next, Coronado looked for another area thought to be full of gold, a land called Quivira. The group went northeast of the Zunis into what is now Kansas. However, they found no gold or other riches. In 1542, they returned to Mexico.

Hernando de Soto was another Spanish explorer who wanted to find gold. In 1539, de Soto led his group to present-day Florida. They went north into what is now Georgia and the Carolinas. They fought and killed many Native Americans, but did not find much gold.

The group then traveled through what are now Tennessee and Alabama. They fought a large battle with Native Americans near Mobile Bay in Alabama, and many men were killed. Next de Soto traveled through the region now known as Mississippi, but once again failed to discover gold.

In 1541, the group pushed westward until they reached the Mississippi River. De Soto and his men were most likely the first Europeans to see the river. They crossed the river and traveled into what are now Arkansas and Oklahoma.

A portrait of Hernando de Soto, the Spanish explorer who led a group of men through southeastern America in search of gold. De Soto and his group were probably the first Europeans to see the Mississippi River.

De Soto Falls, near Lookout Mountain, Alabama, were named after Hernando de Soto.

In 1542, the explorers headed east, crossing the Mississippi River one more time. They turned south into present-day Louisiana, where Hernando de Soto died of fever. He never found the gold he was seeking.

Hernando de Alarcón also led a group of Spanish explorers. They sailed up the Gulf of California in hopes of finding gold. From there they sailed north, exploring the Colorado River, but found nothing. Garcia López de Córdenas led another Spanish group that wanted to find gold. They were the first Europeans to see the Grand Canyon. However, they did not find gold, either.

The Spanish never looked for gold in most of the Great Plains states. In fact, there were no major expeditions in the area until the Lewis and Clark Expedition in 1804.

THE NORTHWEST PASSAGE

For hundreds of years, Europeans believed there was a water route through North America that stretched from the Atlantic Ocean to the Pacific Ocean. They called the route the Northwest Passage. Europeans believed that the country controlling this waterway would control business such as fur trading between Asia and Europe. Controlling this trade would make that country rich.

Several English explorers tried to find a passage through North America. In 1497, John Cabot looked for the passage. In 1578, Humphrey Gilbert searched for it. In 1776, John Cook made an attempt. None of these men found the passage.

In 1800, Spain owned the land that many thought contained the Northwest Passage. This huge area was called Louisiana, or the Louisiana Territory. (Today's state of Louisiana is much smaller.) That year, Spain gave Louisiana to France. Three years later President Thomas Jefferson bought Louisiana for the United States from France, spending $15 million for around 850,000 square miles (2,201,500 sq km) of land. The size of the United States nearly doubled.

President Jefferson wanted somebody to look for the Northwest Passage. He had a scientist's curiosity to learn,

and also wanted his country to control the waterway. The Louisiana Purchase made it possible for President Jefferson to send explorers to probe the land west of the Mississippi River and perhaps find the Northwest Passage. If they did not find the passage, they could at least study the land, its plants, animals, and people.

Meriwether Lewis

President Jefferson picked Captain Meriwether Lewis to explore the Louisiana Territory. Lewis asked William Clark to help. Both men had been on the frontier. They were good, intelligent leaders, and had fought in the Revolutionary War.

Jefferson allowed the expedition to take soldiers on the trip for protection. Other team members included hunters, carpenters, and cooks, all of whom had to be in good health and unmarried. They also had to have lived on the frontier.

By the time the expedition was finally ready, Lewis and Clark had assembled a small group of men. After the expedition began, they decided they needed more men and hired some along the way. They ended up with 30 to 40 men.

The official title of Lewis and Clark's group was the Corps of Discovery. However, most people today call it the Lewis and Clark Expedition.

William Clark

THE CORPS OF DISCOVERY

On May 14, 1804, Lewis and Clark's Corps of Discovery left St. Louis, Missouri. They had a keelboat and two pirogues, which looked like large rowboats. They traveled north up the Missouri River.

They took barrels of flour, fat, and salted pork. (Salted pork is preserved so it will not spoil.) They brought supplies like candles, rifles, and medicine.

They packed gifts to give to Native Americans they would meet on the journey. Some of the gifts were basic things, like iron kettles, or scissors and thread that the Native Americans could use to produce clothing.

Many of the gifts were decorative. The corps took glass beads for the Native Americans to sew on their clothing. And since the Native Americans had no way to make colorful ribbons or mirrors, the corps took plenty of both items on the expedition.

Although the explorers met many friendly Native Americans, the journey was not without hardship. In August, Sergeant Charles Floyd died of a sudden illness. Lewis and Clark buried Floyd's body on top of a hill near modern-day Sioux City, Iowa. Others on the expedition had many injuries and illnesses, but Sergeant Floyd was the only person to die.

Lewis and Clark meet with Native Americans.

Lewis and Clark went farther north on the Missouri River. They met a group of people called Yanktons, who were part of the Dakota nation of Native Americans. The Yanktons were friendly to Lewis and Clark.

The next group of Dakotas were not as friendly. These were Teton Dakotas, who acted as if they might attack Lewis and Clark. However, they eventually let the expedition pass through the area.

By late fall, Lewis and Clark were in the land that today we call North Dakota. They were near another group of

Native Americans called Mandans. Lewis and Clark built a camp called Fort Mandan and spent the winter there.

That winter was terribly cold. The Missouri River froze. The temperature dropped to –45 degrees Fahrenheit (–43 Celsius). Many snowstorms assaulted the land. During the winter, Lewis and Clark spent their time talking with the Mandans about the land that lay to the west. However, Lewis and Clark had to wait until spring to continue their expedition.

In the spring of 1805, Lewis and Clark left Fort Mandan to continue looking for the Northwest Passage. The keelboat, with a small group of men, and Lewis and

Fort Mandan, North Dakota

Clark's written reports, went back to St. Louis, Missouri. The group also brought back plant and animal samples.

Three new people, whom Lewis and Clark met while staying with the Mandans, joined the expedition. One was a French fur trapper named Toussaint Charbonneau. His wife and baby also joined the group. The baby's name was Jean Baptiste. The trapper's wife's name was Sacagawea.

Sacagawea, also called Bird Woman, was about 16 years old. She was a Shoshone Native American. Another group of Native Americans, called the Hidatsa, had kidnapped her and sold her to Charbonneau. She knew the land where Lewis and Clark wanted to travel and spoke the Shoshone language. She agreed to guide Lewis and Clark to the great mountains in the West.

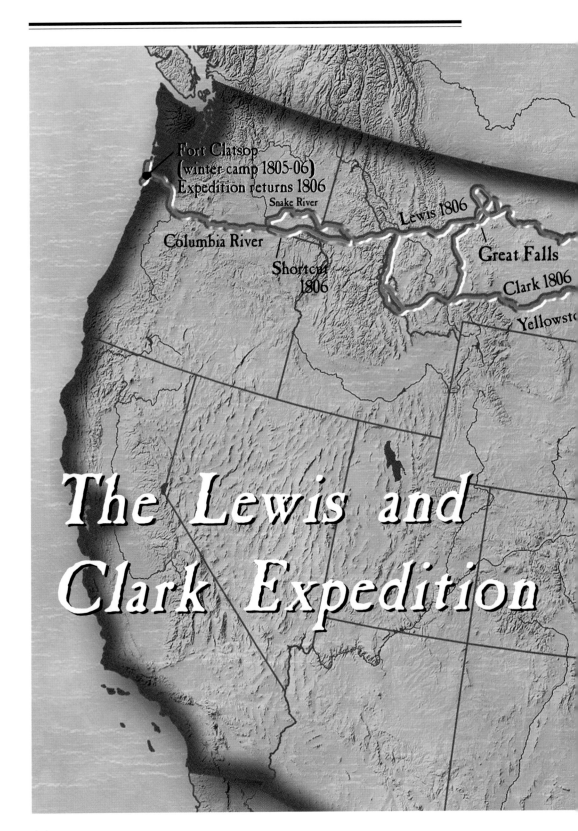

Fort Clatsop
(winter camp 1805-06)
Expedition returns 1806
Snake River

Columbia River

Lewis 1806

Great Falls

Shortcut
1806

Clark 1806

Yellowsto

The Lewis and
Clark Expedition

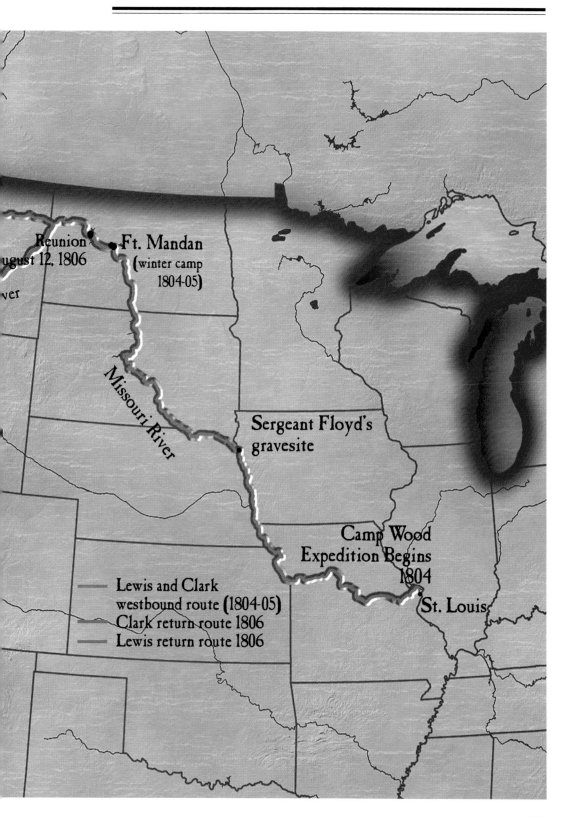

Reunion
ugust 12, 1806

ver

Ft. Mandan
(winter camp
1804-05)

Missouri River

Sergeant Floyd's
gravesite

Camp Wood
Expedition Begins
1804

St. Louis

Lewis and Clark
westbound route (1804-05)
Clark return route 1806
Lewis return route 1806

Sacagawea guides Lewis and Clark through the Rockies.

THE GREAT UNKNOWN

Soon after leaving Fort Mandan, Lewis and Clark came to the mouth of the Yellowstone River. Only Native Americans had gone farther. Lewis and Clark kept going north and west. In June, the group reached the Great Falls of the Missouri River, found in today's Montana.

Since the group couldn't sail up the falls, they had to carry their canoes and supplies through rugged land. They found a lot of rattlesnakes. Cactus needles pierced their moccasins. Grizzly bears attacked the group. The trip around the falls took about a month.

After their land trip, the group traveled on the river again and saw the foothills of the Rocky Mountains. Sacagawea said she recognized the area. She said they would soon come to a place where three rivers came together. This place was called the Three Forks.

At the end of July, Lewis and Clark arrived at the Three Forks. This was the beginning of the Missouri River. Lewis and Clark took the fork that headed southwest. Sacagawea recognized the land and said they would soon find her people, the Shoshones.

Lewis and Clark split up for a short time. Lewis and his men soon met a few Shoshone Native Americans, who alerted their leader about the explorers. A few days later, Clark, Sacagawea, and the rest of the corps met up with Lewis again. Sacagawea knew the Shoshone leader—he was her brother. During this time, Lewis and Clark crossed the continental divide.

After a short stay, the expedition left the Shoshones. The Shoshones traded goods for horses. They also sent a guide with Lewis and Clark.

Lewis and Clark headed west toward the Pacific Ocean. They struggled through snow and rainstorms. They had difficulties traveling across the mountains. They had little to eat and soon became weak. Some of the men fell ill.

Finally, in the early fall of 1805, they were over the mountains. They soon met a group of Native Americans called the Nez Percé, who were helpful to the explorers. They gave them food and helped Lewis and Clark build new

Men dressed as explorers re-create the Lewis and Clark trail.

canoes, which the expedition would need to travel on the Clearwater River through what is now called Idaho.

Lewis and Clark navigated the Clearwater River until it emptied into the Snake River, found in present-day Washington. Then they canoed down the Snake River into the Columbia River, which they followed until they were a few miles from the Pacific Ocean. There, they stopped and built a fort, which they named after the Clatsop Native Americans who lived in the area.

Lewis and Clark stayed in Fort Clatsop through the winter. The winter was not as terrible as previous winters had been. However, rain fell regularly, and they had difficulty finding enough food to eat.

Lewis and Clark spent 18 months going from St. Louis, Missouri, to Fort Clatsop. They had crossed the Rocky

Rolling hills dotted with sagebrush extend below Lemhi Pass, Montana, a route used by the Lewis and Clark Expedition.

A replica of Fort Clatsop, near Astoria, Oregon.

Mountains. They had seen things only Native Americans had seen before.

Lewis and Clark traveled back to St. Louis in just six months. The group had been gone more than two years and four months, and traveled about 8,000 miles (12,872 km). Many people thought everybody on the expedition had died.

Lewis and Clark's Corps of Discovery was the first group of non-Native Americans to start at St. Louis, Missouri, and go to the Pacific Ocean in the Pacific Northwest. Though they had not discovered a Northwest Passage, they found several ways to cross the Rocky Mountains. They made friends with Native Americans, and obtained a great deal of knowledge about the plants, animals, land, and people of the Louisiana Territory.

EXPLORING THE MISSISSIPPI

L eaders in the United States government wanted the people who lived in the newly purchased Louisiana Territory to know that the U.S. owned the land. The government also was curious about the land and wanted to know where the Mississippi River began. In 1805, while Lewis and Clark were still gone, General James Wilkinson sent Zebulon Pike to find the beginning of the Mississippi River.

Pike was just a boy when he became a cadet in his father's army company. At age 20, he became an army lieutenant. For several years, he served in the frontier army.

On August 9, 1805, Pike took a party of 20 soldiers to find the beginning of the Mississippi River. They left St. Louis in a 70-foot (21-m) keelboat and headed north.

Zebulon Pike was an American army officer and explorer.

Zebulon Pike traveled along this stretch of the upper Mississippi River.

In September, they met a group of Dakota Native Americans. Pike made a treaty with the group's leaders.

A short time later, Pike had to stop using the keelboat, which was now too big for sailing on the river. Instead of the keelboat, Pike and his men used smaller boats and continued their northern journey.

Even though winter was approaching, Pike kept going. At what is now Little Falls, Minnesota, Pike built a camp for some of his men. He and a smaller group of men kept moving. They had to build sleds to carry their supplies over the snow and ice.

General Wilkinson had told Pike to find the beginning of the Mississippi River. He had also told Pike to tell everybody in the area that the United States owned the land. Canadian fur trappers from the Northwest Company, a fur-trading company, helped Pike and his men find food and make snowshoes. Despite their kindness, Pike had to order the Canadians to be loyal to the United States and to fly the American flag above their fur posts. The trappers were now on American land. Pike also ordered the Canadians to pay American duties.

In time, Pike found Cass Lake. He believed the lake to be the beginning of the Mississippi River. On April 30, 1806, Pike and his men returned to St. Louis.

Pike's trip was a fair success, even though the United States Senate voted down his treaty with the Dakota. Also, Canadians failed to pay American duties, and Cass Lake was not the beginning of the Mississippi River. Pike, however, provided valuable information about the upper Mississippi River.

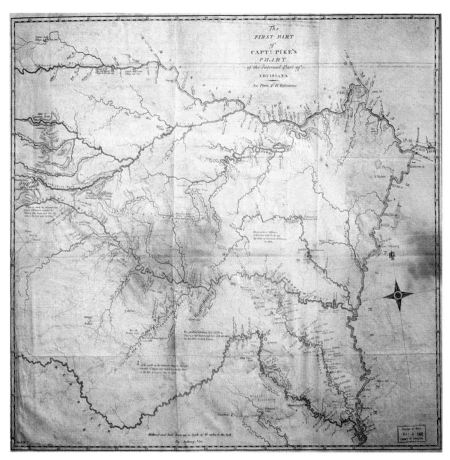

This map of the river systems of the Midwest and South is based on the accounts of Zebulon Pike.

PIKE NEVER CLIMBS HIS PEAK

America knew Spain had armies in the southwest part of the Louisiana Territory. However, their troop strength was unknown. So, President Jefferson sent Zebulon Pike to find out.

In 1806, Pike and his men left St. Louis. They traveled up the Missouri River to the Osage River, then kept going west. Eventually, they came to some villages of the Osage Native Americans.

Pike then traveled north, and soon came to the villages of the Pawnee Native Americans. The Pawnees were unfriendly. Spanish soldiers had visited the villages not long before, and had warned the Pawnees not to deal with the Americans.

In late November, Pike could see the Rocky Mountains. He and three of his men tried to climb the tallest mountain, but they did not make it to the top. Pike never tried to climb the mountain again. Today, the mountain is called Pikes Peak.

Winter came and Pike and his men were not prepared for the cold temperatures. They only had light cotton uniforms. These were summer uniforms and weren't made for cold weather.

Pikes Peak rises over the surrounding woodlands.

The cold weather caused frostbite, and six men had gangrene. Pike made a winter camp near Royal Gorge Canyon in Colorado for the men who were too sick to continue. In January 1807, Pike traveled with the remaining men across the Sangre de Cristo Mountains.

When they reached the Rio Conejus, a tributary of the Rio Grande, the men built a fort. They were now in Spanish Territory.

Soon a Spanish army patrol arrested Pike and his men. The patrol took Pike to Santa Fe. At the time, Americans were not allowed in Santa Fe. The Spanish did not want Americans to know anything about the city or the land around it. Eventually, the Spanish freed Pike and his men.

The Spanish kept Pike's maps and notes. However, Pike remembered enough for a report. Pike wrote about the desert-like prairies of the Great Plains. He thought no crops could grow in the dry soil. The few trees that he saw were small and they only grew near creeks or rivers. To Pike, the prairie seemed almost like a desert.

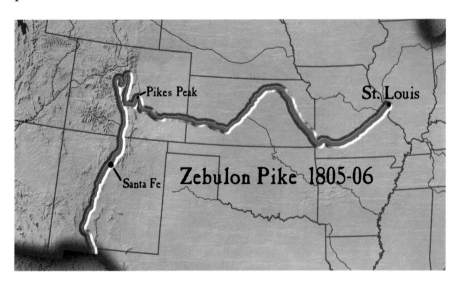

THE GREAT AMERICAN DESERT

In 1820, almost 15 years after Pike searched for the Red River, another group of men went to find the Red River and its source.

Army Major Stephen Long and 20 other men left Council Bluffs (in present-day Iowa) and traveled along the Platte River. They went into the Rocky Mountains and saw the summit of a mountain that they named Longs Peak. About two weeks later, they came upon the tall mountain that Pike and three of his men had tried to climb. Edwin James, one of the scientists of the group, led a small group of men up 14,000 feet (4,267 m) to reach the mountaintop.

Long divided his men into two groups. One group went down the Arkansas River. Long and his group searched for the origin of the Red River.

Long crossed the Purgatoire and Cimarron Rivers. He found a wide stream that flowed east. He thought it was the Red River, but it flowed into the Arkansas River. He then knew it was the Canadian River.

By the middle of September, both groups had arrived in Fort Smith, Arkansas. Neither group had found the Red River or its source.

Major Long reported that the area was like a desert. He claimed the land could not be planted, and that Americans could not live on it. Long drew a map. He called the present-day Great Plains the Great American Desert.

Few Americans settled in the Great Plains. They passed through the area, or simply went around it. Americans believed the area was a desert. They clung to this belief for many years.

A herd of bison graze on a restored prairie in the Walnut Creek National Wildlife Refuge, near Prairie City, Iowa.

INTERNET SITES

http://pbs.org/lewisandclark/

PBS Online's companion Web site to the Ken Burns film, *Lewis and Clark: The Journey of the Corps of Discovery*. The site has information on the Corps of Discovery and Native Americans, provides an expedition timeline, maps, and even includes a Lewis and Clark screen saver.

http://www.kcmuseum.com/explor05.html

This Web page provides information on explorer Zebulon Pike. Maintained by the Kansas City Museum, this Web site also has information on other early American explorers, including Lewis and Clark, Stephen Long, and Father Pierre Jean DeSmet.

These sites are subject to change. Go to your favorite search engine and type in "American explorers" for more sites.

PASS IT ON

History buffs: educate readers around the country by passing on information you've learned about early American explorers. Share your little-known facts and interesting stories. We want to hear from you!

To get posted on the ABDO Publishing Company Web site, email us at "History@abdopub.com"

Visit the ABDO Publishing Company Web site at:
www.abdopub.com

GLOSSARY

Continental divide: An area of high ground on a continent. River systems on each side of this high ground flow in opposite directions.

Corps of Discovery: The official name of the Lewis and Clark Expedition.

Duty: A tax on goods brought in and out of the United States.

Frostbite: An injury to skin and tissue caused by exposure to freezing temperatures.

Gangrene: Decay of tissue in a part of the body due to loss of blood supply.

Great Plains: The land from the Rocky Mountains to just west of the Mississippi River, and from the Rio Grande to the delta of the MacKenzie River in Canada.

Keelboat: A riverboat with a keel but no sails, used for carrying freight.

Louisiana Territory: Land bought by the United States from France. The area went from the Gulf of Mexico to the Canadian border, and from the Mississippi River to the Rocky Mountains.

New Spain: The same area as modern-day Mexico.

Northwest Passage: An imagined waterway across North America that linked the Atlantic and Pacific Oceans.

Quivira: An area that legends said had a lot of gold and riches.

Seven Cities of Cibola: Seven mythical cities north of the Rio Grande River. Legends claimed they had a lot of gold.

Zunis: Native Americans living in New Mexico. Coronado believed the Zunis possessed a lot of gold.

At the Fort Clatsop National Memorial in Oregon, staff members dress in traditional leather outfits and partake in activities of the time. This member is in a replica of the fort built by Lewis and Clark.

INDEX

05.12-03-19

Borrowers Are Responsible
For Lost Or Damaged Materials